101 Surprising Tips to PROMOTE YOUR BOOK

When & How to Build Hype

Mila Johansen

101 Surprising Tips to
PROMOTE YOUR BOOK
By Mila Johansen

Published by Mila Johansen
with Sierra Muses Press
Copyright © 2020 Mila Johansen

All rights reserved. No part of this publication may be reproduced or transmitted in any form or by electronic or mechanical means, including photocopy, recording, information storage and retrieval system, or digital media without written permission from the publisher, except in the case of brief quotations embodied in critical articles and reviews.

Book Design: Mila Johansen

Cover Design: Mariah Miller

Photo of Mila Johansen by Sandy Brooke

Produced in the United States of America

Other books by Mila Johansen:

From Cowgirl to Congress
Journey of a Suffragist on the Front Lines

The Cinderella Monologues - 1st & 2nd Editions
Inspiring Stories of Women Finding Courage & Success
Do you want to tell your story?

Recipes From The Garden Goddesses
For Cuisine, Health & Beauty

A Dog's Best Friend
Dog Training for Real Dogs and Their People

101 Theatre Games
For Drama Teachers, Classroom Teachers & Directors

50 Scenes to Go and Twenty Monologues for Show
For Drama Teachers, Classroom Teachers & Directors

22 Plays and Musicals in Modular Time Lengths
available at classicswithatwist.com

Mila, a seasoned speaker, is available to speak on your stage, podcast, event or summit.

Check out all of Mila's amazing workshops, books and resources at:

MilaJohansen.com

Chapters

Forward by Eric Lofholm .... *i*

1	Best Time to Build Hype	1
2	Write It! Just Do It!	3
3	Social Media Overview—Pick Two	7
4	Facebook	9
5	Twitter	15
6	Other Platforms	19
7	Swag and Shutterfly	23
8	Early Readings	25
9	Your Author Website	27
10	To Blog or Not to Blog	29
11	Email	31
12	Use Fiverr or Hire an Expert	33
13	Amazon Setup and Then On To Ingram?	35
14	Take a Chance and Send it Out	39
15	Set Up Lectures	41
16	To Zoom or Not To Zoom	43
17	Books Beget Book Sales	45
18	Book Clubs Are a Gold Mine	47
19	Podcasting is Where It's At	49
20	Shocking, Bold Promotional Tips	51
21	No Fear—Let's Go For It Gretzky!	53
22	Extra: The Fussy Librarian Formula	55

List of Common Abbreviations for Writers 57
Computer Shortcut Keys and their Functions 59
Writer's Conferences 60
About Mila Johansen 61
About Eric Lofholm 62

Foreword
by Eric Lofholm

Writing the short book to use as a tool can be a great advantage to any professional person or business. So many people want to write a book but are blocked by thinking it has to be a long book. I make it part of my business to encourage business professionals to write their short book. It's attainable and puts you in the center of your field as an expert.

The short book can be your flag, your business card—your giveaway to draw in customers and followers to your orbit. It can also be a way to generate funds. Your short book can be an outline for your future longer book.

And now with all the advantages that Amazon offers to make the process easy—anyone can become an author.

This book, *101 Surprising Tips to Promote Your Book*, is a perfect example of "the short book" concept, as well as a very useful tool to refer to when promoting your own book/books.

Mila Johansen is the author of several books but never thought about writing a "short book" until she took my one day course in "how to write a book in a day."

Mila is also a writing coach who encourages everyone to "just do it". Put the pen on the page, fingers on the keyboard and write! So many surprising and refreshing ideas are presented in this book that will enhance the sales of any author.

Everyone has at least one book waiting to come out onto the written page. Go for it!

Chapter 1

Best Time to Build Hype

Live as if you were to die tomorrow.
Learn as if you were to live forever.

~ Mahatma Gandhi

So, you're writing a book, or you want to write a book, or you have already written a book. Yay! Celebration! How are you planning to promote your book and get it out to the public?

The best time to start building hype for your book was a year ago. The next best time is TODAY. The point is—you don't want to wait until the book is published to start promoting or you will be late to the game.

Right now, authors are expected to advertise their own books whether traditionally published or self-published. But for many, this process seems insurmountable and a great mystery.

No longer—*101 Surprising Tips to Promote Your Book* is here to the rescue! Ta da!

"What will it cost?" you ask. Believe it or not, it can cost you nothing. Or, with some investment, you can find resources to help you get through the parts you don't want to do yourself: editing, book covers, set up, etc.

"How hard is it to do?" you ask. Each step by itself is simple and available to everyone. This book will help you through each step. Don't be afraid to push buttons and try things out. No fear. Check out the tutorials on YouTube.

To inspire you: Harvard put out a study that showed whenever we learn something which seems tough and challenges our brain—we are preventing Alzheimer's. So, every computer skill you learn takes you one more step away from senility.

Chapter 2

Write It! Just Do It!

To begin, give yourself permission to write a bad book. Then revise until it's not a bad book.

~ Barbara Kingsolver

"Keep your butt in the seat." That is the mantra circling the writer's world right now. Another is, "20 minutes a day is all we ask." Just think—20 minutes a day of writing could add up to a book. I tell my students—even 5 minutes a day!

I have to tell you a story. My mother tricked me into becoming a writer. Yep—she tricked me—thank goodness. She told me to write one sentence a day for a month. Well, it's almost impossible to write just one sentence. I would end up with a whole page or more. So, by the end of the month—I was a writer.

I write best in the morning, but often find myself writing at all hours of the day. For instance, when I get a free moment, or an idea comes to me and must be written down. Even a few minutes at a time adds up. Some people are better at night when all is quiet. The famous female 19th century French novelist, George Sand, started writing at midnight and didn't stop until sunrise. There are no rules except "keep your butt in the seat." Just do it!

I met one writer who sits and writes from 8:00 am to noon every day. He sets his own rule that all of those hours have to be new writing—no hiding behind editing or research. Then if he wants to write more, or do editing and research, he can do so later in the day. He puts out a book a month. The famous science fiction writer, Isaac Asimov, wrote for the same hours each day.

I read about another successful writer who went to a certain place in the world. He just sat there and wandered around and observed, for about a year, before he knew what his next book would be about.

You don't have to be perfect—we have editors. My grammar and spelling were atrocious when I first started writing, but I didn't let those weaknesses stop me. The important thing is to write. Get it down as fast as you can and fix it later. Don't try to be perfect in your first draft. Let it be messy and unorganized—just don't stop. And . . . you don't have to start at the beginning. Start with any idea that comes to you and work your way through it.

Which brings us to an important question. Are you a pantser or an outliner? Traditionally, I have always been a "pantser"— I write by the seat of my pants, making it all up on the spot. I have used outlines a couple of times, but I found, if I left it wide open, different characters and situations would appear that I never would have thought of by approaching it in an organized way. Those characters and situations brought unexpected layers and depth to my stories.

Yet, there is a lot to be said for outlining. Especially for "How To" books or nonfiction books. I have met several fiction writers who swear by outlining and is the only way they are able to function. Most are open to changes and ideas when they occur.

Over the years, I have done most of my writing on my computer. But lately, I have gone back to pen and paper. I find my writing acquires more layers and depth if I hand write it. In many college classes—they have banned computers, asking the students to hand write their notes. Studies show that people retain the information on handwritten notes substantially more than when typed on a computer.

So now, on to having fun promoting yourself!

With its weight and solidity, a book signals to the world that there are ideas worth preserving in a form that carries heft, and takes up space; by its touchability, a book signals the importance of our engagement in an arena external to and larger than ourselves.

~ Steven L. Carter

Chapter 3

Social Media Overview—Pick Two!

You are what you share.

~ Charles Leadbeater

Don't be afraid of what you don't know. We all started somewhere and wherever you are in the cyber world is right where you are—perfect! You may already have some social media skills. You may not have any.

You might want to hire someone to do it for you. I encourage you to learn at least one social media platform yourself. Remember, anything that frustrates you helps prevent Alzheimer's. And then there are those of you who are already well-versed in more than one, or all the social media platforms.

Pick Two! One of my mentors told me to pick two social media platforms and concentrate on those. I get great response from Facebook. Facebook has so many attributes and is a great way to build a following. I was stuck at 56 followers on Twitter for almost eight years, until I discovered a formula that brought me up to 7,000 in nine months. I will share this formula with you in the Twitter chapter.

YouTube, Instagram, LinkedIn and Pinterest are also viable places to promote your book. My advice is to sign up for all of them, see which ones you get the most play from, and then pick two.

The most important advice I can give is to encourage you is to ask questions every day on the Internet. If you don't know how to do any of the following tasks—ask Google. Usually, a short tutorial will pop up on the top left-hand side of the page instructing you exactly how to accomplish your task. And use YouTube tutorials. There are several for just about anything you want to learn.

Heads up! I have had several agents and publishers ask me how many followers I have on Twitter, Facebook and other platforms. I am so glad that I have worked on it ahead of time and can report a healthy number. Don't get me wrong, you can publish without the social media numbers, but it sometimes can make the difference of being accepted or not.

One representative told me she was in New York presenting an array of books. Her client, interested in two of them, asked, "Which author has the most social media followers?" They immediately chose the book written by the author who had the most. In today's market, they want to make certain you are a sure bet. By the way, self-help books and how-to books are still all the rage.

As I understand it, names cannot be copyrighted. My friend wrote a book and there were so many books with the same name—Heartwood—on Amazon. So, I encouraged her to break it into two words: Heart Wood—which there were less of. She did it.

Your MS (Manuscript) is copyrighted as soon as you type the words on your computer. I have a trick. As soon as I come up with a title, I search to see if it's out there. If it is, I tweak the title a little. Then I make a Twitter and Facebook page with the name so that when others search to see if the name is taken, they find my sites. So far, it has worked. I then use those sites to start promoting.

Free! All of the above is free. Repeat after me . . . FREE!

Chapter 4

Facebook

Honestly, if everyone likes what you say something is wrong with your message.

~ Ashley Ormon

Besides Twitter, Facebook (FB), in my opinion, is the most flexible format for promoting a book. You can make a very attractive page within minutes and start posting.

Your Facebook page is a useful tool to build an audience and keep friends, family and supporters updated about your progress. They will be an enthusiastic audience for when you publish. Ask them to leave a review if you are on Amazon. Reviews from actual buyers are the ones that count and improve your ratings.

You can also join Facebook writer's groups to promote your book. Join them before your book comes out if possible. I am a member of over fifty FB writer's and book groups in anticipation of my next publication.

If your book is in a specialty category, like midwifery, construction, childcare, accounting, etc. Join all the FB community groups you can in that genre and you will have a ready audience. Post on your own timeline until you get the drill, then share from there.

Things to do on Facebook:

1. Check your Security Status in two places: next to 3 dots on timeline and arrow at top right of timeline and arrow on Home Page.

2. Pick the right name for your Business Page and Community Page—Name of Book.

3. Start a Business Page if you don't already have one, automatically linked to your personal page.

4. List website and any other pertinent links. Include contact information if desired.

5. Insert photos into banner and icon spaces – update any time.

6. Find images in your own archive and on-line to include in posts – Use free graphics/photos.

7. Create posts with blurbs about your book or business and ways to draw people in.

8. Join and post on community sites that are related to your subject. Writers!

9. Learn how to schedule posts on business site. Note: There is an edit feature for any post.

10. Create your "Story" and "About" sections. Look at other FB sites for ideas.

11. Learn to create an event! Very exciting for personal or Business! Book launch. Book announcement. Updates.

12. Create short (about a minute) videos on Facebook Live. Do it often for results.

13. Explore the power of Giveaways.

14. Create Events then invite all your friends. Post event on groups in that subject range. Ask people to "Share".

15. Stay out of FB "jail" by only posting to 10 community groups at a time.

16. Make lots of friends and then invite them to "Like" your author page.

17. Bumping – Look it up. It means to comment on a post later to bump it back to top of page.

18. FB Congeniality is the name of the game. Be friendly and polite at all times. No politics.

19. FB Messenger is a great way to go directly to your friends and potential buyers. Once.

20. Communicate and "Like" other people's post. It makes them like you—builds algorithms

21. Share your FB Author page on other social media platforms, asking for "Likes".

Deep Dives:
1. Post about once or twice a week on each Community FB site. Check Private Messages (PMs) regularly! The best times to post to get the most response is 6:45-7:15am or from 4:00-5:00pm. Saturday mornings or Friday evenings are the very best days. But it is good to vary it from week to week. If wanting a wider audience besides local, post before 6:00am and before 5:00pm. I belong to over 300 Facebook community sites for various subjects. I suggest joining ten groups to start.

2. Create posts and blurbs with photos to appeal to potential customers. Each week could feature a different image and different approach through wording. Save all your images in a file and all your blurbs in another to reuse.

3. Looking good. Now post something on your business page every day or every other day. Every other post

should be promotion for what you do, and the other one something of interest from another web site. (Self-improvement, ideas, recipes, inspiration, nature photos—other) These cross-build your algorithms and the postings bring people to your page.

4. The next step, once you like how everything is looking, is to invite your friends "on the right" to like your page. You now need to generate fans that will see what you post. Invite "Friends" the same times listed above for ultimate exposure. Find ways to invite people to "Like" your page. Ask close friends to invite their friends—same way. Ask people in a post once in a while to "Like" your page. ***Only do this at the optimum posting times listed above.

5. Once you post an ad up on your business page, "share" that on the local FB community groups or for a broader audience— once a week at the opportune times. Post one and then go and see how it looks before posting more – make changes as needed. Sometimes you have to copy the words and insert them with each post. There is an edit option.

6. Look at other people's posts to get ideas. Read other's "Story" & "About" sections.

7. FB ads are helpful once in a while. Set a budget, i.e., $30.00. Posts are often just as effective.

8. Create an Event for your book launch.

9. Direct messaging is another great avenue. Before or after your general posts—before is suggested—private message everyone you can on FB announcing that your book is available for purchase. Then your follow up

Facebook

posts on your timeline and business page will be further reminders to everyone in general.

10. If your launch is close to a holiday—capitalize on it. Frame your book launch around that upcoming holiday. My new book came out close to Mother's Day. So, I wrote on every posting, "Great Gift for Mother's Day." Give potential buyers ideas. Christmas, Valentine's Day, Mother's Day, Father's Day or other.

You may want to make a posting schedule to include all of the above. Something like this:

- Private message everyone
- Post on Timeline
- Post on Business page
- Post in Community FB groups
- Bump 8-12 hours later to put back at top of pages
- Take out a FB ad

Good job, the more you do it, the easier it will become!

ASK the Internet how to do anything and don't forget about YouTube tutorials.

Chapter 5

Twitter (aka: X)

Men of few words are the best men.
~ William Shakespeare, Henry V

Twitter (now known as "X") is a fairly friendly format and is probably the best format for writers. There is a very substantial, active community of writers supporting writers. Every day two or more people ask for books they can buy to read and support other writers.

Someone will say, "I want to support writers, so I am going to buy five books. Spam me your books, people." Or some such message. Of course when they say they will buy five books, they usually mean eBooks, which makes buying five affordable. You want people to read your eBooks, it means your books are being read and then maybe talked about.

Again, if possible, start building up your Twitter following before your book comes out. Better to be "late to the game" than to not show up at all. Start when you can.

Twitter is a great exercise in economy of words. Each message is limited to 280 characters including spaces, punctuation and #hashtags. You will be surprised how many words are fillers and you can live without.

Hashtags are a universal way to attract people to your post. Use these popular ones to attract writers and readers: #writingcommunity #amwriting #5amwritersclub #writersnetwork #readers #WritersLift #readers. Notice hashtags that others are using and copy.

Three words:
1) Participate
2) Participate
3) Participate

I created this formula especially for writers. If you do this at least once a day for at least ten minutes a day, you should see your numbers rise quickly. Participate in Follow Fridays and Shameless Promotion Saturdays.

Formula:
1. Like other people's posts (Heart)
2. Retweet other people's tweets
3. Comment
4. Post your own post—280 characters max

Participate:
Interact with others and respond to their posts, questions and requests. Add a gif (Active Pic), favorite, comment, poll. Post your book link or description, blog, answer questions about your MC (Main Character). Answer questions about anything.

Ways to attract followers:
1. Follow—many will follow you right back

2. Create Polls once you have some followers. Get ideas from others.

3. Call to action. Do this—do that. Ask questions.

4. Pin your most important post – some will retweet it for you!

5. I mainly follow writers. I say in comments. "I love to follow writers." That statement gets me lots of followers.

Twitter (aka: X)

Don't answer messages unless it pertains to you and your project.

Secret: Retweet notices, ideas and connections that will help your book sales. Your profile is a useful storage area.

Big Opportunity: Four times a year there is something called Pitch Wars. #PitchWars and PitMad. #pitchwars is a mentoring program, ending in an agent showcase. pitchwars.org.

#PitMad is a pitch party to hopefully attract an agent on Twitter where writers tweet a 280-character pitch for their completed, polished, unpublished manuscripts. Agents and editors make requests by liking/favoriting the tweeted pitch. Every unagented writer is welcomed to pitch. Pin your pitch during that period.

Here Are Some Useful Writer Abbreviations
More at End of the Book

MS – Manuscript

MC – Main character

WC – Word Count

POV – Point of View

POD – Print on Demand

AGT – Agent

PRO – Protagonist

ANT – Antagonist

QL – Query Letter

NF – Non-fiction

HF – Historical Fiction

MF – Mainstream Fiction

WF – Women's Fiction

YA – Young Adult

NA – New Adult

MG – Middle grade

PB – Picture Book

SP – Speculative Fiction

RO – Romance

TH – Thriller

UF – Urban Fantasy

SFF – Science Fiction Fantasy

FF – Flash Fiction or Follow Friday

CNF – Creative non-fiction

PB – Paperback

Chapter 6

Other Platforms

The pessimist sees difficulty in every opportunity, the optimist sees opportunity in every difficulty.

~ Winston Churchill

There are new platforms popping up every day and it can get very confusing, even to seasoned social media experts. Try to keep your focus on the main two or three you chose. Again, I suggest Twitter and Facebook. If you choose more than two, try to stick to the more popular suspects. You will probably get more attention and attract more followers on those that have been around for a while and have proven records.

LinkedIn offers many substantial attributes. It's a little slower on the up draw when it comes to collecting a following. It seems to attract the professional, business crowd, which can be very useful and might be the perfect audience for your book. I have a substantial following on LinkedIn but only post there once in a while. Like other social media platforms, posting every day builds presence.

Secret: One expedient technique for posting on multiple platforms is to create one post on Facebook and then copy and paste it onto all the others. This can be a ten-minute project, once you get the hang of it. Or, find one of the online services that allow you to do scheduled posts on multiple platforms.

Instagram can be an effective site to sell on or at least to build hype. I have some friends who actually do most of their sales from Instagram and do very well. Again, posting every day is the key. Take a tutorial.

Etsy! Here is one that will *surprise* you. I use Etsy as a website to sell my books. It's easy and painless to set up and offers a beautiful store-type format. Etsy is very organized with many wonderful attributes. I have used it to receive payments for workshops, book bundles and many other items. It's another place to put your books up for sale. The *secret* to sales on Etsy is to post something every day and fill in all 13 search words. Let's say you only have one book. Copy that post every day. Your entire store page will be repeats of the same book.

You buy your stash of books from Amazon for your author price and have them on hand. You steer potential buyers there on social media and, voila, for less percentage than Amazon takes (Etsy takes 8%) you are making sales.

Ebay is another very credible format to post your books.

Pinterest. Yes, I said Pinterest. Some people are getting very good traction by creating pages to go with their subject matter. Go on the Pinterest site to see how others are posting and using it.

Not a platform, but. . . I have found going to writer's conferences, taking workshops online, and joining groups in all forms to be extremely valuable. I have met an unlimited amount of people who I can network with. We help, encourage and learn from each other. So many of my resources came from these opportunities.

Without fail, every time I attend any kind of meeting or seminar, I come away with one to several "Ah ha" life-changing strategies. Without all of these incredible resources, I would still be floundering in my own stone age of partial knowledge.

Still, there is so much for me to learn and absorb. I give myself permission to not stress and just take my time, while challenging myself to reach for new goals and increase my computer skills. There is a complete treasure trove of opportunity for each and every one of us.

*When a book leaves its author's desk it changes.
Even before anyone has read it, before eyes other than
its creator's have looked upon a single phrase,
it is irretrievably altered. It has become a book that can
be read, that no longer belongs to its maker.
It has acquired, in a sense, free will. It will make its
journey through the world and there is no longer
anything the author can do about it. Even he, as
he looks at its sentences, reads them differently now that
they can be read by others. They look like
different sentences. The book has gone out into the world
and the world has remade it.*

~ Salman Rushdie

Chapter 7

Swag and Shutterfly

*In every day, there are 1,440 minutes.
That means we have 1,440 daily opportunities
to make a positive impact.*

~ Les Brown

You need to start stock piling SWAG now. What is SWAG you ask? I didn't know and looked it up on the Internet for this chapter. SWAG stands for "Stuff We All Get." No kidding. If you have ever attended big conferences like Comic Con—you come home with plenty of SWAG—free promotional stuff. Some of it is just ho-hum and some of it can be worth hun-dreds of dollars. My daughter attended an event with Conan O'Brien where they handed out bobble-heads of him. She sold hers on eBay, before the event was over, for $200.00.

Your SWAG for your book doesn't need to cost you a lot of money. But sometimes you can sell your own SWAG.

Okay, no more business cards. Repeat after me: "No more business cards." Instead, order bookmarks with your book description and your cover, and/or your photo, name, website and email. You can design one side or, for a little bit more—print on two sides. The reason to pass out bookmarks is:

1. People keep them and use them and . . .
2. They make an impression with size.

I didn't have a cover yet and I later changed the name of my book, but giving out bookmarks helped people to remember and ask me about it later. I've ordered three batches and handed out over 750. The last batch had the final title of the book printed on them.

I have found a secret place to build up your SWAG stockpile. Shutterfly. Get the phone app and also sign up on your computer—Shutterfly puts out free promotional items about once a week. You only have to pay shipping. I looked into buying many of the same items from other companies and they cost up to ten times more. For instance, the 3 x 5 refrigerator magnets would cost $5.00 and up. On Shutterfly, I pay $1.00 each.

These are the items I order with photos about the book and/or the cover to hand out at speaking engagements, seminars and book readings to build hype.

1. Magnets 3"x 5" People love them
2. Return Labels
3. Canvas Bags
4. Playing Cards—hand them out at events, use them to conduct raffles
5. Calendars
6. Free 6" book every month
7. Free 8" book about every 3 months

The up-and-coming item to order, with your book cover printed on it, are fans. Just simple, thin cardboard fans on a stick. You've seen them. Several companies are offering them. Hand them out at summer events indoors and out. People love being handed a fan in warm weather. You can put your book on the front and more info on the back. Don't forget to add in a sentence on front where to buy: Available on Amazon or Available at Your Local Bookstore. Include your website.

Chapter 8

Early Readings

You can never get a cup of tea large enough or a book long enough to suit me.

~ C.S. Lewis

There are plenty of opportunities to read parts of your unfinished book and excite readers for the future launch. Join writer's groups, book clubs, men's or women's clubs and more.

Offer to read as often as possible and in any place you can think of. In our writer's group, at every launch, we have readings from the works in progress, as well as from the actual books being launched.

I have also posted short excerpts from an upcoming book on my Facebook Author page as a teaser to keep the interest going. You could also read excerpts on Facebook Live.

Another technique, writers have used for years, is to offer one chapter at a time online until the book is finished—for a fee or for free.

I finished my first book seventy-six years ago. I offered it to every publisher on the English-speaking earth I had ever heard of. Their refusals were unanimous: and it did not get into print until, fifty years later, publishers would publish anything that had my name on it.

~ George Bernard Shaw

Chapter 9

Your Author Website

I have always imagined that Paradise will be a kind of library.

~ Jorge Luis Borges

It is important to have an author website. You can pay for a professional to design it or you can do it yourself on one of the many website builder programs.

If you go to Fiverr.com, there are experts from all over the world who will create a beautiful, functioning site for a fraction of what you would pay otherwise. Check out all the offerings at Fiverr.com. You can get editing, a book cover, book design and even someone to upload it onto Amazon. Fiverr is an incredible resource for just about anything you want done and it is, for the most part, affordable.

Some of the easy-to-use website builders for you to do it yourself:

1. Wix
2. WordPress—Elementor and Beaver Builder are free templates and easy to use
3. WordPress suggested for a one-time fee is Divi—easy to use
4. Weebly
5. imcreator.com
6. Squarespace
7. Many more

Look at other author websites to get an idea of a design that appeals to you. Gather ideas about images, content, headings and more. Think about if you want to be monetized to receive payments. PayPal is an easy solution for receiving payments. Do you want an email sign up option? Do you want to have a give away? I would suggest a button that takes them to Amazon or any other site where your book is sold.

Ideas for Headings (Tabs) under your banner from actual websites:

Home   Books   Lectures   Author Bio   Contact

Meet Author   Programs   Events Calendar   Daily Call   Contact

Home   Book   About   Actor   Director   Playwright   Teacher   Contact

For books, most authors use their own name as their website name. Get a professional photo (head shot) taken of yourself. Repeat after me, "**professional**". Most of us have friends who are photographers, or you can hire one. It makes a big difference.

Chapter 10

To Blog or Not to Blog

Life isn't about finding yourself
Life is about creating yourself.

~ George Bernard Shaw

That is the question. How could it hurt? Blogging is a great way to get your message out. Do you have time? That is the real question. I always say **YES** to everything and then back off if I have to. The power of YES is very potent.

Many websites come with an automatic blog option. Try it. You might like it. It might even become your next book. I have a friend who has done hundreds of very effective, on subject blog posts. I suggested to her that they could make up her next book. In fact, more than one book. She had never thought of that idea and was thrilled. A reverse way to think about it is to use your chapters for your blog once your book comes out.

It can be a little difficult finding consistent readers. But who knows, look what happened in the book *Julie and Julia*! Her blog became a national sensation and a movie. Taking the time to write a blog can always lead to somewhere. Maybe even think of it as your next book written in segments. So pay attention to the content and quality as you go.

Another way to steer people to your blog is to offer a giveaway. Think of something for free that you can afford to give away. That is how one friend I know collects emails. She gives something of value when subscribers fill out the email form.

Giveaways invite people into your orbit.

Participating on Twitter and Facebook can also be a way to entice readers to your blog. Often, one of your followers will say, "Hey everybody, post your blog address and let's all read each other's blogs." Or you can instigate a blog party.

One easy way to promote your blog, is to be a guest writer on someone else's blog. Contrary to the rumors, guest posts aren't dead. The secret, however, is to write posts for blogs aimed at readers of your genre of book.

Don't forget to put a short bio (one or two sentences) at the bottom of the post, to point people to your work. Something like:

Mila Johansen is the author of From Cowgirl to Congress, along with several other books and 22 plays that circle the globe. You can find her books at milajohansen.com.

Just start and see what happens. It's all an adventure.

Chapter 11

Email

If I don't get at least one e-mail very ten minutes, I feel unloved. Even junk mail makes me feel seen.

~ Chris Abani

Believe it or not, Email Marketing is not dead! Email Marketing is up to 40 times more effective than social media, according to a study. The same study also shows that the buying process happens 3 times faster than on social media. Wow! Who knew? So keep gathering those emails—they are gold.

MailChimp is a great format for email. There are many. Kartra is another program that does many things along with an email program. And then of course there's GoDaddy and Aweber. Explore the various options and ask friends which they recommend.

Send out a series of emails starting with a "Save the Date" for your launch. You don't want to bombard your email audience so they opt out before the book is actually available. Send one announcing the launch date, including any launch events. After the book is solid and published on Amazon or other formats, then send out a series of emails—always with an opt out option.

Email content should be light and friendly—chatty. A picture is worth a thousand words. Change your email subject for each send out. You can put a direct link to Amazon or any other site to buy the book. You may choose to insert a "Buy" link. Get a friend to help you or look up how to do it.

*Good cover design is not only about beauty...
it's a visual sales pitch. It's your first contact with
a potential reader. Your cover only has around
3 seconds to catch a browsing reader's attention.
You want to stand out and make them pause and
consider, and read the synopsis.*

~ Eeva Lancaster

Chapter 12

Use Fiverr or Hire an Expert

Always listen to experts. They'll tell you what can't be done, and why. Then do it.

~ Robert A. Heinlein

I have used the site called Fiverr for several aspects of my publishing. It is a site where all sorts of services are offered. Some are as little as $5.00 (hence the name Fiverr) and then the price goes up from there. You can go to the site and check out different offerings from book covers, to editing, to book layout, to Kindle upload. NOTE: I do suggest that you also ask, beforehand, if they give you the final product so you will always own it and have it in your own files.

There are also several sites on Facebook with cover artists and most of them are very affordable.

Here are a few of them on FB:
- Book Covers and Cover Artists
- Premade Book Covers and Artists Worldwide
- Book Cover Design Marketplace

My own examples:
- I paid $500.00 for a cover from a local professional
- I paid $40.00 on Fiverr for a cover for another book.
- I paid $100.00 for another cover for another book.

I have actually paid two different cover artists on Fiverr, when they were reasonably priced, to see which result I liked best. You can afford to do that on Fiverr. Freelancer.com is another option to explore.

Or you could go the professional route, which can cost quite a bit more, but be totally worth it in the long run. Please, please, PLEASE have your book professionally edited. I've pick up too many self-published books that have not been properly edited and it makes me say, "Ouch!"

Editing can cost anywhere from $1,000 to 2,500 and is well worth the cost. That may be the direction you want to take. If you can spend money on one thing, I suggest you find a good editor.

I would steer clear of vanity publishing houses unless you meet a really good one you can trust. They offer an appetizing publishing package that can cost anywhere from $2,500 to 10,000 or more!

Another way to explore your options, is to shop your book around to agents and publishing houses first, to see if you can land a contract. My sage advice is to shotgun your queries to agents—at least ten at a time. Don't wait for each one to get back to you. Agents all say that simultaneous submissions are accepted. Publishing houses can vary on that protocol. Then after 200 rejections (no kidding—one man was finally accepted after 200 tries) then consider self-publishing.

Many people do very well with self-publishing and for many—it is their first choice. One of my mentors told us that the more books you have published—the more sales you will make.

Chapter 13

Amazon Set Up and Then On to Ingram?

*Never trust anyone who has not
brought a book with them.*

~ Lemony Snicket

Here is the magic formula. When your book is finished—edited and set up with all the trimmings, upload it to your Amazon account and have samples sent to you for proofing. Usually, it only takes a few days to get the trial runs back, which is expedient. Secret: We found that if you uploaded it on a Friday or early on a Saturday, it somehow comes back quicker. What I'm trying to say is, don't wait until Monday if it's ready on a weekend.

This back and forth might need to happen several times until you see that your book looks like you want it to. This is the beauty of Amazon. For my recent book, because it has many photos, it took eight sample runs. For my friend, hers only took two samples because she had no images—just prose.

Order at least four copies each time so you can hand them to beta readers and others, to proof for final edits, with a fresh set of eyes. You will be surprised at what they find and suggest. Only make changes you agree with. **Note:** Save the trial run books to hand out later.

My sample copies, at 300 pages, cost a whopping $4.35 each with free shipping. If you have a very short book, it should cost anywhere from $2.50 to $3.50. **Warning:** if you have any color photos or images, besides the cover, your sample could cost twice as much each. Keep it simple if you can.

Work on crafting an effective bio. **Secret**: Be sure to include any relevant search words, that apply to your subject matter, in the first two or three sentences. Name-dropping is a great technique to use for search words.

Have a professional photograph taken of yourself. Repeat after me, "professional". We all have friends who are photographers, or you can hire one. It makes a big difference.

There is another amazing attribute of Amazon. Let's say you launch your book, and then you find a mistake, or you think of something you want to change or add. Make the appropriate changes, upload the new PDF and voila, your manuscript is even better.

Now, after some sales on Amazon, and if you are happy with your book, you may want to also put it on Ingram. There are many advantages to having your book on both Amazon and Ingram.

Bookstores and libraries like to order directly from Ingram. You would need to buy the book, have them shipped to you and then either take them in person or ship them. According to the experts, you still have to approach bookstores, through email or direct mail, to let them know about your book. Bookstores will also be able to see your book listed with Ingram. Ingram can be tricky—get help.

An alternative plan! If your goal is to have your book carried by bookstores and libraries, you may want to upload your book on Ingram Spark first, before Amazon. This simplifies things by requiring you to have only one ISBN number. Ingram Spark also takes care of submitting your book to Amazon, GoodReads, and many other places. It's a one-stop shop! If you are only working with Amazon, ignore this last paragraph.

Amazon offers you an ISBN number for your book. If you go the Ingram route, you will need to buy an ISBN number from a company online called Bowker. You will buy ten at a time and need a different one for each book format: paperback, hardcover, audio. Buy them early to avoid delays.

Another way to play the game is to offer the hardcover or paperback for a number of weeks before you post the eBook and then move on to offer the audiobook. That way everyone in your waiting audience will buy the book to have in their homes and you bring in more money to help with the expenditures. You want your family and friends to have the physical copy on their bookshelf.

Pay attention. Ask everyone you know who buys a book to leave a review. The more reviews the higher in rank your book goes. But the reviews that really count are from actual buyers on Amazon. You can request reviews in all your advertising also.

Note: We discovered that when we ordered books to a P.O. Box—delivery took longer—sometimes twice as long. We received books in a shorter turnaround time when delivered to a physical address. Tell your friends about that when they buy.

The next move is the next chapter!

My mantra, thinking of authors, is that it is good to create, better to create and publish, and best to create, publish, and monetize. May every author be successful in all these matters.

~ Lee Foster

Chapter 14

Take a Chance—Send It Out!

Maybe it won't work out. But maybe seeing if it does will be the best adventure ever.

~ Emma Westbrook

Competition is fierce out there in the world of books right now. So, we have to pull out all the tricks and take surprising action to get noticed. I'm planning on sending my book out to all the agents that didn't accept it so they can see I mean what I say. The next time, I approach them with a book, they might take me seriously and give me a chance. It's a way to get their attention.

I would love to live in the time that Margaret Mitchell was discovered. An agent for a publishing house traveled south to Atlanta, by train, to hunt up books and writers. He accidently met Margaret and asked her if she knew anyone who was a writer. She told him she sort of had a book. Very interested, he pressed her to let him read it. She reluctantly handed him a suitcase with a huge mash of papers that he had to sort through. And the rest is history. But those days are gone with the wind.

Make a list of local and no- so-local places you would like to talk about your book: radio, women's or men's clubs, book clubs, podcasts and more. Think subject matter. I have a friend who helped develop and grow rare, organic grains like kamut. He just finished an entire year traveling around the country, giving presentations and selling his book.

Invest in a box of your own books. Send a book to each prospect at the USPS book rate with a cover letter saying you would be honored to speak on their program. Be sure and use your return label, stationery and stamps that go along with your book cover.

Hint: You can buy large quantities of 9" x 12", or any size, bubble wrap envelopes on eBay for a very reasonable price.

Note: You may have to send the cover letter separately—they do not allow any correspondence in same envelope as mail going book rate.

No fear. Send it out to anyone you can think of.

Chapter 15

Set Up Lectures

We were all convinced that we had to speak, write, and publish as quickly as possible and as much as possible and that this was necessary for the good of mankind.

~ Leo Tolstoy

One of the best ways to sell your book is in-person, when speaking at bookstores, clubs, libraries, museums, house parties, tea parties, colleges, classrooms, conventions and anywhere you can think of. The listeners usually feel inspired, and sometimes obligated, to buy your book on the spot. That does mean that you need to have a box or two of books with you, which you should have at all times anyway.

Contact all your local groups and offer to be a guest at one of their meetings. If you know you will be in a certain area, for instance, visiting family or attending a convention, contact the groups in that area and bring some books along. Or you could even have them shipped to your destination.

PowerPoint presentations are a great way to show images, graphs and/or sentences that reiterate the points you are trying to make. If you are presenting a memoir, pictures are still worth a thousand words.

Zoom is an effective and useful way to speak remotely to groups out of your area or locally when needed. Offer that option in your email or cover letter.

Note: During Covid, I had to pivot and offer all of my lectures online—on Zoom and via Podcasts. It turned out to be an amazing opportunity. I spoke all over the world, rather than just in my own community, and the U.S.A. as I had originally planned

Last, but not least—if appropriate—make an offer at the end of in-person or online presentations. Offer a discount for the book if purchased immediately. Or offer a free eBook or PDF. PDFs can be different items, even a recipe from your book or something that goes along with your theme. If yours is a how-to book, offer a free one-on-one phone call to promote any classes you are planning to offer.

Hint: Offer your talk/lecture in various time segments:

- The 10-Minute Speech
- The 20-Minute Speech
- The 40-Minute Speech
- The 1-Hour Speech
- More than an hour with reading excerpts
- An entire day seminar

By offering a variety of options, you have a better chance of being booked. I also offer my PowerPoint as an option in case a particular group or space does not support a PowerPoint presentation.

You may have several subjects you could speak on besides your current book topic. On your website or Facebook, compile a list of presentations you offer along with suggested lengths—under a banner heading for easy access. These same subjects could also be offered to Podcast shows.

Chapter 16

To Zoom Or Not to Zoom

Speak to me: I will spend my lifetime trying to understand you.

~ *Kamand Kojouri*

The short answer is . . . YES! Or use a similar program—there are many. Zoom is easy and now most people are familiar with it.

Zoom is an effective and useful way to speak remotely to groups out of your area, or even locally. Offer that option in your email or cover letter. Some groups, believe it or not, have not fully joined the digital age, so you might have to set up the Zoom meeting yourself. You would invite them and tell them to sign up for Zoom or whatever other format you might be familiar with.

If you don't already know how to conduct a meeting on Zoom, get together with a friend and practice. It's easy. Be sure to record every meeting you have, because some of them will be good enough to upload to YouTube or other platforms. It's also a great option for remote family members and friends to see your presentation.

If you can, create a PowerPoint to go along with your lecture. Zoom or a webinar program lets you show your computer screen and people can follow along. Be sure to dress for the part. Professional is best. It's a good idea to practice your speech beforehand. You can even record it by yourself on Zoom. Note: Zoom allows 40 min time slots without signing up for a payment plan. If you are going to use it often and for longer time slots, you might want to sign up for the lower payment plan. As options, you might check into Google Hangouts and Microsoft Teams as well as other services. Blue Jean is another one that offers more for free.

Last but not least—if appropriate—make an offer at the end of in-person or online presentations. Offer a discount for the book if purchased that day. If yours is a how-to book, offer a free one-on-one phone call, or a discount to a paid Zoom call, or a free tip sheet—or anything else you can think of.

The great aspect of Zoom is that you can record your Zoom call. So, you might want to practice your presentation by yourself to see what you look like—what your background looks like—what angle you look your best in. Pay special attention to lighting. There are some really good, reasonably priced 6" and 21" ring lights on Amazon and eBay. Even just one 6" ring light can make a huge difference in your appearance.

Then, you can review the recording, and if you like how it turned out, save it to share with friends and family who are remote or could not attend any of your Zoom presentations.

Another very useful attribute of prerecording yourself, is that you then have a professional video of your lecture that you can use in many ways. If you are inclined to offer a class or presentation on Teachable, Thinkific, or one of the other teaching platforms, you have it ready. You could then develop an entire class around your book with specific class materials and handouts. Note: One of the best ways to learn Teachable or Thinkific is to take a class. There are free classes and many tutorials.

Chapter 17

Books Beget Book Sales

So many books, so little time.

~ Frank Zappa

I have a mentor who says the more books you have on Amazon and/or other formats, the more books you will sell. At the time, he had 25 books on Amazon and was in the process of writing more. He said the more books he published, the better all of his books sold.

He developed a relationship with a writing partner that he shares all of his earnings with. This could be any type of arrangement, one person writes the first draft, and the second person cleans it up and edits it. Or each takes every other chapter in a self-help book or . . . the possibilities are endless.

For certain kinds of books there could be several books within a book: the short version, the long version, the children's version, and the young adult version.

If your book is especially long, you might think about dividing it into two, or even three, books. With the short attention spans of our society today, long books are no longer the fashion.

A short how-to book could be an icebreaker that you give away for free or super cheap, almost like a business card. That same book could be an outline for the longer version.

Amazon requires that a book has to be at least 38 pages long. That is a very thin paperback. You can also offer it as a PDF for instant download. That way there is not a postage fee—no muss, no fuss.

By the way, how-to and self-help books are still the rage and are selling well. The most popular genres that Podcasters are searching for are business how-to's, women's empowerment, health and advice along with self-help gurus.

If you are an on-line instructor, a great way to teach is from your own book. It can be a very short book that you provide as your class textbook. It can even be your perfect guide for making your Zoom video with your PowerPoint for programs such as Thinkific. A short book can be the flag that you wave to attract students.

Chapter 18

Book Clubs Are a Gold Mine

"Outside of a dog, a book is man's best friend."

~ Groucho Marx

There are millions of book club members in the U.S.A. and dozens of book clubs in your surrounding areas that you can reach out to read excerpts or to speak about your book. The beauty of book clubs is that many of them ask their members to buy your book and read it before you arrive for your presentation. It's a great way to get your book into surrounding area bookstores.

The more book clubs you offer to read or speak at, the more guaranteed books sales you will generate. Bring books with you and you will likely sell more of them on the spot. The advantageous thing about selling your books in person, is that your profit is higher than when sold online or through a publisher.

According to *Forbes*, book clubs are thriving in the Internet era. And lately more and more are popping up everywhere. You can offer to present in person or on the Internet through Zoom, or one of the many other video platforms. Search Google for "The best book clubs in the United States." You will come across many types of lists of clubs that you can write to or call to set up a reading or a presentation.

When you know you are scheduled at a book club in your area, be sure to make sure your local bookstores have plenty of books in stock for the members to purchase before your presentation.

Try and give plenty of lead-time so they can slot you in—most only meet once a month. It is totally acceptable to suggest that they organize a special meeting to accommodate you when visiting a certain area due to time constraint. This goes for presentations at any kind of club or gathering. Book clubs are a waiting audience for you.

If you love to write, start a blog.
If you love to talk, start a podcast.
If you love to solve problems, start a business.
If you love freedom, do what you love.

~ Maxime Lagacé

Chapter 19

Podcasting Is Where It's At

Be yourself; everyone else is already taken.
~ Oscar Wilde

There are two ways to participate in podcasting. If you have ever given a radio interview, it is exactly the same thing, except longer. You can be a guest on podcasts, or you can host a podcast yourself.

Being interviewed as a guest on a podcast is completely painless and a wonderful way to broaden the outreach of your book/books. The host will send you a link for you to select or dial into. You just answer questions and speak about what you already know. Since you are not seen, you can have notes in hand or on your computer in case you need to refer to them for names, dates or any other information. **Note**: Some podcasts do both video and audio.

Learn the host's name beforehand so you can use it through-out the podcast. Try to leave breathing room for when the host wants to speak or ask another question. If the host does not stop you, keep going on with your story and info. Be sure to try to insert the name of your book through-out the podcast, especially at the beginning and end. Be gracious and thank the host in the beginning and again at the end. Then also, send a thank you note by email afterward.

The host will usually ask you to tell your friends and social media following about the podcast to garner more listeners. This is a great time to have a good following in place, as many hosts choose people to interview based on number of followers.

Usually, the host will send you a link to the podcast afterward for you to share. This is also a great advertising tool for you to use to promote your book on FB, YouTube, Website, Twitter and more. Some podcasters have huge followings and will be invaluable to book sales.

You could also create your own podcast. It's not difficult. You might want to ask a friend to help you set it up or watch YouTube tutorials—or just try it yourself.

There are many free podcast-hosting sites like Podbean, Buzzsprout, Speaker, Podiant and Anchor. I suggest you get a recommendation from someone or use one that you were a guest on.

There are several Podcast groups on Facebook you might choose to join. Often, members of these groups are looking for people to host. You can ask questions like: What podcast platform do you use or suggest? What kind of mic do you use? Can I use the built-in mic on my computer? Who would like to be a guest on my podcast?

I suggest you try out your first few podcasts on friends and family, to get your broadcast legs. You may be surprised at how professional your first broadcast can be. It may even be something you save as a promotional tool.

You don't always have to interview someone. It can be a monologue. Some podcasters trade—I'll interview you and you interview me. **Hint**: Be open to modifying your subject. I found that focusing on the journey of my grandmother from a troubled childhood to becoming a professional woman attracted more invitations than focusing on just her successes. Again, self-help and empowerment is the rage.

Whether you are a guest or host—have fun with it. Be relaxed and easy. Breathe and always be ten minutes early.

Chapter 20

Shocking, Bold Promotional Tips

I have not failed. I've just found 10,000 ways that won't work.

~ Thomas A. Edison

Go for it! What do you have to lose? Shameless self-promotion is where it's at! Whether you are traditionally or self-published, promoting your own book is the wise thing to do. I have listed the expected ways for you to build your following, and now I will give you some shocking ideas that I have gathered from various sources that are proven to work!

1. Give valuable ideas away for free. Become the expert.
2. Brag about others and help them in any way you can.
3. Make magnets and put them on anything metal, wherever you go.
4. Put a large magnet on your car—include the title of your book, and where it is available.
5. Cover your car with small magnets with cover/info for people to take.
6. Ask for referrals and recommendations.
7. Send books to celebrities, radio show hosts, TV stars
8. Give away books at events, on Twitter, radio, Facebook, or in gift baskets.

9. Ask someone with a big following, local or not, to write the foreword.
10. Reverse shoplifting—leave your book in stores next to famous name books.
11. Throw a big party and feed everyone—read excerpts and sign your book.
12. Make t-shirts and give them away.
13. Create fans and/or bottles of water to give away at events with cover and book info.
14. Use prweb.com to send press releases to 30,000 or 40,000 web sites.
15. Name all your social media pages with your book title.
16. Sign up for a booth or table at conventions and events.
17. Exercise fiercely to keep your energy up and put on your brave.

Don't underestimate the power of SWAG. One man told of a bold move he made to get his book on everyone's radar. He applied to have it included in the spectacular gift basket of SWAG, worth $225,000, given to each of the stars at the Oscars. They accepted. His book became a bestseller and is now being made into a movie.

Chapter 21

No Fear—
Let's Go For It Gretzky!

You miss 100% of the chances you don't take.
~ Wayne Gretzky

Now that you have your bag of tricks—all of the tools in the previous chapters—you can start them all at once or one at a time. The main idea is to start! Whether you started last year, yesterday or today—just start! Whether you do one of these things or all—just start!

I often tell my students that it's like being in a paper bag and we have to work our way out. Start with one thing. Start with the easiest or start with the hardest. Think about each task as if you're putting together a puzzle and have fun with it. The mist will clear, and the task will no longer be an enigma. It will become second nature. I promise, after you do the task enough times, you will be able to show others how to do it—pay it forward. One of the best ways to learn is to show or teach others.

I've said it before, exercise every day to keep up your energy and put on your brave. I walk every day to rev up and get going. Exercise erases the cobwebs and the doubts.

Don't forget to use your most valuable resources, friends, family and social groups. Most of us aren't raising barns anymore, but there are other ways in which we can help one another.

Enlist those around you for brainstorming sessions, mailings, local book launches, word of mouth, posting on their own social media sites, and anything else you can ask them for. Tap into their expertise. Maybe each person in your volunteer team can take on one task. Most people will be happy to help and be honored that you asked.

Tit for tat may be where it's at. You help me and I will help you. I may be good at Facebook and you might know how to build websites. Let's trade and help each other.

You are brave.
You are courageous.
Every day is an adventure!

REPEAT AFTER ME:

I am brave.
I am courageous.
Every day is an adventure!

Chapter 22

Extra: The Fussy Librarian Formula

There are many online opportunities to promote your book. You will have to pick and choose to see which ones to use, and how they fit into your budget. Most help build hype and at least pay for themselves. One of the best sites I have found is Fussy Librarian. The great advantage of The Fussy Librarian is this is an easy way to get your book onto the Amazon Bestseller List—maybe even into the very first slot of the "Top 100".

Here is the formula. Go into your KDP book page and go to "Bookshelf". Then to the right of your book is a box marked "Promote and Advertise". Select it. You will have two choices. "Kindle Countdown Deal" and "Free Book Promotion". Both are for your eBook. Read about both.

I suggest you do "Free Book Promotion". I have found that you get much greater response when the eBook is free.

Some people say, "I don't want to give away my book for free." And I tell them that the people taking you up on the "free offer" are generally buyers that will never hear of your book otherwise, and it builds hype. Also, if you do choose "Kindle Countdown Deal", you will only get a few cents per book anyway.

Some people I know gave away 1,000 to 2,000 or more eBooks using Fussy Librarian. A few writers noticed a huge jump in sales after the giveaway. There are no promises, but this is a tried-and-true method to get your book noticed and read. And it is almost guaranteed that you will become a Bestseller, which is great advertising tool.

The giveaway can last up to 5 days. I suggest you do all five days and start on a Wednesday, and then schedule your one-day giveaway or sale on Fussy Librarian on a busy day like Saturday.

On the first day of the giveaway or sale, advertise it on your social media sites and ask your friends and family to help by reposting. Then, send out an email to your lists and ask them to help you reach the Bestseller List by purchasing your book for the $1 sale, or by choosing the free giveaway. People will love to help you with this, and it will build your response.

Then on your KDP page, go to "Reports" throughout the day and watch your numbers rise.

Once you get on the Bestseller List in your subject area, take a screenshot to share with followers and family. You can find your seller status on your book's main page under product details, near the bottom. Click on the first subject area to be taken to the page where your book is pictured with the other books it ranks with. It's very exciting!

Below is an example of what happened to my rankings with a free giveaway of *From Cowgirl to Congress* on the first day.

Bestsellers Rank: Free in Kindle Store
- #1 in Biographies of Social Activists
- #9 in Historical Biographies (Kindle Store)

And by the 2nd day, both categories were #1.

Bestsellers Rank: Free in Kindle Store
- #1 in Biographies of Social Activists
- #1 in Historical Biographies (Kindle Store)

Common Abbreviations for Writers

I don't use these when writing to agents and publishers. They are good to know for Twitter and for communicating with other writers. I concentrate on the most useful ones.

WIP – Work in Progress
MS – Manuscript
MC – Main character
WC – Word Count
POV – Point of View
POD – Print on Demand
AGT – Agent
PRO – Protagonist
ANT – Antagonist
QL – Query Letter
NF – Non-fiction
HF – Historical Fiction
MF – Mainstream Fiction
WF – Women's Fiction
YA - Young Adult
NA – New Adult
MG - Middle grade
PB – Picture Book
SP – Speculative Fiction
RO – Romance
TH – Thriller
UF – Urban Fantasy
SFF – Science Fiction Fantasy
FF – Flash Fiction or Follow Friday
CNF – Creative non-fiction

Common Abbreviations for Writers continued

PB – Paperback
R&R – Revise and resubmit
Indie – Independent
BG – Bad Guy
BS – Back Story
GN – Graphic Novel
RI – Romantic Interest
F – Fantasy
HR - Horror
SF – Science Fiction
CP - Critique Partner
AU – Alternate Universe
NaNoWrMo – National Novel Writing Month
Pantser – No Outline
Plotter – Makes an Outline of Book
Plantser – Combination
VSS – Very Short Story
TBR – To Be Read
Comp – Comparable Titles
ARC – Advanced Reader's Copy
MSWL – Manuscript Wish List
BSL – Bestseller List
HEA – Happily Ever After

Computer Shortcut Keys and their Functions

Ctrl on PC = Command on a Mac
Alt = Option on a Mac computer

Ctrl or Command + A: Select all text.

Ctrl + C: Copy selected item.

Ctrl + V: Paste selected item.

Ctrl + X: Cut selected text.

Ctrl + S: Save

Ctrl + B: Bold highlighted selection.

Ctrl + C: Copy selected text.

Ctrl + P: Open the print window.

Ctrl + I: Italic highlighted selection.

Ctrl + U: Underline highlighted selection.

Ctrl + Y: Redo the last action performed.

Ctrl + Z: Undo last action 1-150 times.

These are a few examples of what is available. There are many more you can look up.

Writer's Conferences

Attending Writers Conferences is a great way to make networking contacts. It is also an automatic in with some agents and publishers. Often, you get the option (sometimes for a payment) to meet face to face with agents and/or publishers. It is your big chance to pitch your book.

Here are the 11 of the best writing conferences (according to one list) for authors—look them up on Internet.

1. Author Advantage Live
2. San Francisco Writers Conference
3. San Miguel Writers Conference and Literary Festival
4. Digital Author and Indie Publishing Conference
5. Santa Barbara Writers Conference
6. Sewanee Writers Conference
7. Writer's Digest Annual Conference
8. Writing Day Workshops
9. Middlebury Bread Loaf Writers Conference
10. AWP: Association of Writers and Writing Programs
11. SleuthFest

About – Mila Johansen

Mila Johansen is a public speaker, coach and writer. She enjoys helping entrepreneurs and writers all over the world write and publish their books, making the process easy and accessible. Mila is the best-selling author of 12 books and has written and produced several short screenplays. She also has three thought-provoking, upmarket women's fiction novels in the works. In addition, Mila teaches social media, screenwriting, creative writing, herbology, and public speaking.

Mila published *From Cowgirl to Congress*, a book about her famous suffragette grandmother, Jessie Haver Butler, for the 100th anniversary of women winning the right to vote in August 2020. Jessie was on the front lines of the suffrage movement in Washington D.C. with Carrie Chapman Catt and Alice Paul as the first woman lobbyist. Before that, in 1911, she helped organize the Pulitzer School of Journalism.

Jessie later established speech classes where she taught thousands of women to command the podium. Eleanor Roosevelt endorsed Jessie and opened each of her series of classes with a lecture. When Jessie was in her early nineties, Mila accompanied her as she shared the stage, several times, with Gloria Steinem and Marlo Thomas.

Trained by her grandmother, Mila is a professional public speaker. She lives on her organic citrus ranch in Northern California with her husband, three dogs, and two cats.

More on Mila's courses and books at milajohansen.com

About – Eric Lofholm

Eric Lofholm is the best-selling author of *The System* and is a master sales trainer who has taught over 10,000 students. Eric has helped generate nearly $500 million in revenue over the last two decades.

He honed his skills as a sales trainer for Tony Robbins from 1997 to 1999 before founding his own company, Eric Lofholm International. He offers expert training both for corporate sales departments and individuals who want to improve their sales skills.

In his sequel, *Sales Scripting Mastery*, Eric lays out the seven-step sales scripting method he has used over the last two decades. He walks you step-by-step through the sales scripting process, revealing secrets such as how to script an effective close and how to script responses to sales objections. He follows up with tips on how to get your scripts written faster and how to rehearse and deliver them effectively, so they sound spontaneous. For salesmen, sales trainers, and small business owners looking for an edge in today's struggling economy, this book is a must-read. Both books are available on Amazon.

Learn about Eric at saleschampion.com
Explore all of his books on Amazon.